Job's Journey

By Larry Chkoreff

First Printing Spring 2007
Version 1.5.2-January 2013
ISBN 978-0-9823060-3-1
Copyright © 2005 by Larry Chkoreff
Published by International School of the Bible (ISOB),
Marietta, Georgia, U.S.A.

For information on reproducing this book contact ISOB at:
Email address – info@isob-bible.org
The ISOB web site is www.isob-bible.org.

Unless otherwise indicated, all Scripture quotations are taken from the New King James Version Bible Copyright © 1982 by Thomas Nelson, Inc. When quoted by verse with numbers, the original quote marks were left in place without editing.

Forward

When challenged to write about Job, I have to admit that I had a difficult time coming to grips with the task. I felt for years that the Lord would eventually challenge me. When He finally did I knew that it was He that was calling me, and also, that I could not and would not write a word without hearing from Him for sure.

There are most likely millions of writings and commentaries about Job that have been written for centuries. I have read a few on the web, and while they are very helpful to a point, it just seemed like something was missing. I had heard an audio series back in 1992 on Job from Malcolm Smith, [1] which was very good and anointed. In 2005 I purchased this series again, and it is still anointed and probably the best I have studied yet. Many of the ideas in this booklet are from Dr. Smith's teachings. However, I felt like God wanted to reveal something else.

In this short booklet about Job, I wish to point out that in no way do I claim to have any sort of "total understanding" about the life of Job and his journey with God. When the created being attempts to comprehend his Creator, there will always be something missing. I do believe however as we walk and talk with the Lord that He will progressively show us new things that we can apply in our own lives and share with others. Having said that, I wish to state first that I subscribe to Job 42:3, which says, "Things too wonderful for me to try to understand." I think that we need to approach Job this way. However, I do believe that as we ask the Lord to show us His mysteries, as He deems them to be valuable I do believe that He will reveal many "wonderful" things to us, but perhaps not all.

---

[1] http://www.malcolmsmith.org/home.asp

Job's Journey

People, for centuries have asked the question, "Why do the righteous suffer?"

Why did Job suffer? Many have attempted to come up with formulas about how to live or not live, and formulas about the character of God, so that they may have a neat and tidy doctrine by which to live a "safe life."

Job has several sub issues, many truths, that are not the ultimate TRUTH. These are worth exploring, but if we explore them without first having *the* TRUTH, then we are missing God's purpose for the Book of Job.

I submit that there are many issues that result from God's dealings with Job. However God has put on my heart something beyond the theology of why do the righteous suffer, and what was the cause and affect of Job's suffering, or how he could have avoided it. We are not gong to hit that head on like many commentators. I hesitate to try to "explain" things.

I understand that Job is one of the ancient writings of Scripture, a primitive book.

I believe that God wanted to settle something in the beginning of Scripture; something very elementary about His dealings with man.

I submit that Job is a shadow and a reflection of mankind, yes of you and me.

I believe that what God was after in Job and in all of us is the important issue on which to focus. That bottom line truth I submit is, *God wants to replace "you" with "Him in you."* One of my favorite authors, Watchman Nee, said in one of his books, "*We cannot please God, but Christ has to replace us.*" Christ in us the hope of glory!

As we get into the Scriptures, I will make comments as they progress.

Job 1:1-22 says,

> *"1 There was a man in the land of Uz, whose name was Job; and that man was blameless and upright, and one who feared God and shunned evil.*
>
> *2 And seven sons and three daughters were born to him.*
>
> *3 Also, his possessions were seven thousand sheep, three thousand camels, five hundred yoke of oxen, five hundred female donkeys, and a very large household, so that this man was the greatest of all the people of the East.*
>
> *4 And his sons would go and feast in their houses, each on his appointed day, and would send and invite their three sisters to eat and drink with them.*

Apparently Job had been extremely successful as a businessman and as a man of character.

Later in the Scripture it states that he was not greedy with his money, that he consistently helped the poor, and was generally kind, benevolent, and was a God fearing man. Now remember, he was not a born again person. This was not possible at that time. So here is a man, who in his old "flesh nature" was living beyond what most blessed believers live like today. How many of us can claim this kind of prosperity along with this type of godly character before we met God face to face?

God's testimony about Job in chapters 1 and 2 was amazing. He was quite a man, and yet he was unregenerated. When I compare myself in my own unregenerated state to Job's, I was a terrible mess! Perhaps you were also. Therefore if Job outshined all of us, then even the best of us have many things to learn. There are none righteous.

As we will uncover later in this booklet, Job was self-righteous, not as a Pharisee, but in an honest sort of way that was okay with God for a season. God knew He could trust Job to be His man. However, he knew that all Job had was his good works. He knew little about grace and about God's character.

Quote from Ray C. Steadman [2]

> *The Revised Standard Version says he was blameless, and many who have read that thought it meant that Job was sinless. But it is not the same thing. You can be sinful and still be blameless if you have learned how to handle your sin the way God tells you to. Evidently Job had learned how to handle sin, so, in that sense, he was blameless. I do not think, however, that this is the best translation of the Hebrew word that appears here. It is really a word that means "a complete man." Job was well balanced and the reason he was well balanced was that he feared God. He was not a materialist, he did not just look on life as a means of getting ahead in the world.*

My first premise is therefore, is that there are few, or most likely none of us, as perfect as Job was in his old unregenerated nature.

---

[2] Stedman, Ray C. The Test - Series: Let God be God. 1995 Discovery Publishing - Peninsula Bible Church, 1977

Job is the ultimate standard of what looks good in the life of a man but is really "filthy rags of self-righteousness" to God. None of us were as good as Job, yet God does not count Job's righteous acts as enough. What about you and me?

Job, his friends, and all of us, need a lesson in God's grace.

Grace is not simply excusing sin and overlooking it, real grace comes when God can bring us to a place of brokenness, repentance and then He replaces you with Him!

I submit that this does not usually happen until we reach the end of ourselves and truly "see Him" face to face. At the end of the Book, Job saw God face to face. In Abram's life, God "appeared" to him.

How did God teach Abram his first grace lesson?

All of us, like Abram, have valuable raw character material that needs to be purified. In that perspective God needs to deal with our self-sufficiency, or some call it our "flesh." Sometimes it is difficult for us to discern between the works of the flesh and the wind and grace of God, but God has a way of defining that for us. It is called "breaking."

Abram entered his training period, his preparation for his destiny and purpose. Do not despise your "mountains" your disappointments or failures. God wants to bring His purposes to you by His power, His grace, and He needs to get your self-sufficiency out of the way. Often He cannot do that by doctrine but by experiences.

I will paraphrase what Paul said about grace.

"Look, I know I have been born into privilege even religious privilege, that I have been educated with and by the best. I have performed perfectly in my vocations, I was a real performer, and few people could keep up with me. However, I have noticed something interesting. The fruit

5

that I see in my life and in my ministry is fruit that came from my afflictions. That fruit far surpassed anything all my natural strengths could and did accomplish. I was amazed! His resurrection of my afflictions has produced more fruit than all of my performance! Therefore I long for His resurrection power to work in my life, and I count all other things as "dung." I would rather have Him turn my Junk into Jewels any day!" (reference 1 Corinthians 12, Philippians 3)

Job 1:5 says,

> *5 So it was, when the days of feasting had run their course, that Job would send and sanctify them, and he would rise early in the morning and offer burnt offerings according to the number of them all. For Job said, "It may be that my sons have sinned and cursed God in their hearts." Thus Job did regularly.*

I am not sure about this, but I wonder why it states that Job performed burnt offerings for his children and not for himself. It's just something to consider. Was it a form of self-righteousness?

Job 1:6-7 says,

6 Now there was a day when the sons of God came to present themselves before the LORD, and Satan also came among them.

7 And the LORD said to Satan, "From where do you come?" So Satan answered the LORD and said, "From going to and fro on the earth, and from walking back and forth on it."

Satan has no throne.

He is in no way co-equal to God. He is a vagabond wandering around the universe. However, apparently he did usurp man's access to God in the Garden of Eden.

Jesus won back our place at the throne.

"And He said to them, 'I saw Satan fall like lightning from heaven. Behold, I give you the authority to trample on serpents and scorpions, and over all the power of the enemy, and nothing shall by any means hurt you. Nevertheless do not rejoice in this, that the spirits are subject to you, but rather rejoice because your names are written in heaven'" (Luke 10:18-20).

Jesus is our mediator and high priest. Job needed to discover this. We all do.

"Let us therefore come boldly to the throne of grace, that we may obtain mercy and find grace to help in time of need" (Hebrews 4 16).

God chose Job for an important task.

Job was good; good in morals, he was very talented and therefore prosperous in his self-life. Then why does God not offer all the prosperous people to Satan to consider? God saw Job's heart for Him, which not all prosperous and moral people have. Why should Satan disturb a prosperous worldly person who he already has deceived, who is not attempting to serve God? Why upset the apple cart? I am so glad that God said to Satan, "Have you considered my servant Larry, whose life by the way, is already in your power because of his unregenerated flesh." I am so glad that my worldly prosperity was attacked and thus failed. But God resurrected my prosperity, and me, like He did Job's.

Job 1:8 says,

> *8 Then the LORD said to Satan, "Have you considered My servant Job, that there is none like him on the earth, a blameless and upright man, one who fears God and shuns evil?"*

I submit that God lured Satan into this conflict simply to defeat Satan. If Satan put man down in the Fall, then man through the power of God has to return the defeat to Satan.

Go with me into this scene in Heaven and allow your imagination to travel with mine for a moment.
God sees Satan hanging around the Throne. Satan has the right because he stole it from Adam. But God sees how He can use the adversary's own power to defeat him. God thinks to Himself, "Hmm, here is an opportunity to give Satan what I have in store for him, and at the same time give Job the blessing I have in store for him."

He teases Satan and says, "Then the LORD said to Satan, 'Have you considered My servant Job, that there is none like him on the earth, a blameless and upright man, one who fears God and shuns evil?'" (Job 1:8).

He taunts Satan by bragging about Job. God is trying to get Satan to engage in warfare with Job.

Satan in effect says, "Job looks at you as his heavenly 'bell boy.' He only serves you because you have blessed him." He accuses God as stooping to bribery and he accuses Job as being only a "top line" man[3]. He attacks the character of both Job and God.

Now perhaps that is why God choose Job for this battle. He knew Job was lacking in a lot of things, but He knew Job was a bottom line man. Job was not in this for what he could get from God. He worshipped God just because He is!

Satan in effect says, "Job is only righteous because you have blessed him. Take it away and see what happens."

Perhaps an angel comes to God and says, "Hey Boss, what are You doing here? Job is our man. Please don't unleash Satan on him." God says, "Listen here angel, what I

---

[3] One who is more concerned with his/her own comfort than with the purposes of God and others.

am really saying is, ' Come on Satan, make My day! My servant Job is going to take you on. Then after he defeats you, this will be my model for the Church which is to come.'" The angel says, "Church. What's that?"

"A senseless man does not know, Nor does a fool understand this. When the wicked spring up like grass, And when all the workers of iniquity flourish, It is that they may be destroyed forever" (Psalms 92:6,7).

Job 1:9-11 says,

> *9 So Satan answered the LORD and said, Does Job fear God for nothing?*
>
> *10 "Have You not made a hedge around him, around his household, and around all that he has on every side? You have blessed the work of his hands, and his possessions have increased in the land.*
>
> *11 "But now, stretch out Your hand and touch all that he has, and he will surely curse You to Your face!"*

Satan was railing an accusation against Job and God, proposing that Job only served God for what God could do for him. He proposed that Job had looked at God as some sort of "heavenly genie" who he could manipulate. Satan went on to propose that Job would "dump" God if all the blessings were removed. Satan had challenged God to remove the "hedge" from around him, and then stand back and see how Job would view God.

Job 1:12 says,

> *12 And the LORD said to Satan, "Behold, all that he has is in your power; only do not lay a hand on his person." So Satan went out from the presence of the LORD.*

This verse, 1:12, in my opinion, is where so many people get mixed up about the entire Book of Job.
It appears to me that God was saying, "Behold, look, all that Job has is *already* in your power." I do not see anything about God acknowledging that there was a hedge, or that God had removed it. I see God informing Satan that all of Job's stuff is already in Satan's dominion. God did not have to do anything but to inform Satan of the existing facts.

I surmise this not only by the text in verse 1:12, but also in the totality of Scripture. I do not see anywhere in Scripture that God has put a hedge around someone's "stuff" especially someone who is "walking in the flesh and not in the Spirit." As sons of Adam, everything we have is under the dominion of Satan to begin with. As we encounter God for ourselves, as we really see our weakness and undoneness, then we experience the New Birth, we go through death and resurrection and little by little our lives change from the blessings we can put upon ourselves to the resurrected blessings that God can bestow upon us. Satan cannot then touch those resurrected blessings.

Job had worked out his blessings of "stuff" for himself, under his own power, the power of his natural soul life. Possibly some of the blessings were there because he utilized the principles of God. Today, even secular corporations, which exercise servant leadership, giving, kindness and goodness towards their customers and employees, plug into the principles of God's economy. But they have not plugged into God, as He would want every one to do, even someone such as Job who God treasured.

Job 1:13-22 says,

> *13 Now there was a day when his sons and daughters were eating and drinking wine in their oldest brother's house;*

14 and a messenger came to Job and said, "The oxen were plowing and the donkeys feeding beside them,

15 "when the Sabeans raided them and took them away--indeed they have killed the servants with the edge of the sword; and I alone have escaped to tell you!"

16 While he was still speaking, another also came and said, "The fire of God fell from heaven and burned up the sheep and the servants, and consumed them; and I alone have escaped to tell you!"

17 While he was still speaking, another also came and said, "The Chaldeans formed three bands, raided the camels and took them away, yes, and killed the servants with the edge of the sword; and I alone have escaped to tell you!"

18 While he was still speaking, another also came and said, "Your sons and daughters were eating and drinking wine in their oldest brother's house,

19 "and suddenly a great wind came from across the wilderness and struck the four corners of the house, and it fell on the young people, and they are dead; and I alone have escaped to tell you!"

20 Then Job arose, tore his robe, and shaved his head; and he fell to the ground and worshiped.

21 And he said: "Naked I came from my mother's womb, And naked shall I return there. The LORD gave, and the LORD has taken away; Blessed be the name of the LORD."

22 In all this Job did not sin nor charge God with wrong."

Up to this point, Job did not charge God. However, that was about to change.

Job 2:1-7 says,

"1 Again there was a day when the sons of God came to present themselves before the LORD, and Satan came also among them to present himself before the LORD.

2 And the LORD said to Satan, "From where do you come?" So Satan answered the LORD and said, "From going to and fro on the earth, and from walking back and forth on it."

3 Then the LORD said to Satan, "Have you considered My servant Job, that there is none like him on the earth, a blameless and upright man, one who fears God and shuns evil? And still he holds fast to his integrity, although you incited Me against him, to destroy him without cause."

4 So Satan answered the LORD and said, "Skin for skin! Yes, all that a man has he will give for his life.

5 "But stretch out Your hand now, and touch his bone and his flesh, and he will surely curse You to Your face!"

6 And the LORD said to Satan, "Behold, he is in your hand, but spare his life."

7 So Satan went out from the presence of the LORD, and struck Job with painful boils

*from the sole of his foot to the crown of his
head.*

Here God said, "Behold *he* is in your hand."

In Chapter 1 God said, "All that he *has* is in your hand."
Now God infers that even Job's health is in Satan's hand. I
believe that to be true in every person's life that has not been
regenerated. However, once we have been born again, and
have developed a close relationship with the Lord, this can
no longer be said.

Notice also, that Job's *life* was only in God's hand, not
Satan's. This is important. We pray for the healing of sick
people. We pray in faith, nothing wavering, and believing in
the promises of God. We pray until perhaps the bitter end.
However we are told in this verse that our lives are only in
the hands of God, and that Satan has no dominion over when
we die. Certainly we can, by disobedience and presumption,
live a lifestyle that would bring an "early" death, but even
then, God is in control of our life and death situations.

We are to lay hands on and pray for the sick, without fear
that perhaps they will not be healed. Pray anyway! The
healing is God's job.

One problem with many believers that I have noticed, is
that they are always trying to figure out and explain why
some person did not get healed. That is "too wonderful" to
do. Do not judge another. Fear to judge another as "not
having enough faith." Life is complicated, and God is too far
above us in dimensions and wisdom to try to apply a formula
to someone else's life. Simply keep on judging yourself, stay
in the light, pursue closeness with God, and He will speak
His wonders to you.

Remember, faith comes by hearing God speak. He
cannot speak to you if you're misjudging someone else.
Strive to hear the rhema of God, not just the logos in the

Word. The rhema, or a personalized message from the Word, will bring faith and God will perform that thing. Being presumptuous with God's logos, the general Word, can bring presumption. Again I refer to Job 42:3 which says, "Things too wonderful for me to try to understand."

Mark Rutland tells a story about his mentor in missions, precious Jim Mann. Jim is also the grandfather of a missionary friend of mine. When Jim was lying on a sick bed, in his elder years, he had heard from the Lord that he was being called home. Just then an overzealous Christian came in and with loud shoutings, rebuked the sickness and claimed Jim's healing. He laid a healing cloth on Jim and left. Jim turned to Mark, neatly folded the cloth, and said, "Some people just don't know. He meant well. But God is calling me home."

My grandfather, Spiro Chkoreff, an immigrant from Macedonia in the early 1900s, was lying on his bed in 1933. He was 83. My uncle, his son, was rubbing his feet to keep the circulation strong. Spiro said, "Okay son, you can stop now. Gabriel has come for me. I am leaving." He was swept into glory! My grandfather had planted one of the first Macedonian churches in Detroit. He was a soul winner and lived a life of passion for the Lord.

Job was not well equipped at this time in his life for spiritual warfare.

Job did not know that Satan was behind his suffering. I think he was really confused. His friends "knew" that Job's sin must have been the cause. However we know that Satan was behind the suffering. Are we to simply then go into a state of relaxation, and say, "What will be will be"? No, no. We are called to stand against evil in the face of our circumstances.

I believe that Job's life is a model for us to be overcomers.
I believe that is our vocation in life, as it was the apostle Paul's. When Paul asked God to get rid of his thorns, which were the legalists who were standing against his message of grace, God told him to overcome the evil with His grace. Did Paul just sit back and "put it into God's hands?" No. He became all the more active in fighting his fight of faith. He wrote more epistles, preached harder, and stood for who God was.

Overcoming is what brings real defeat to our satanic enemies.
The Book of Revelation makes it clear that what our vocation is, and what is valuable to God for our lives, is to be overcomers and to overcome our spiritual enemies. I believe that this ancient Book of Job is an early warning system for us to heed. Our job is to face the satanic enemies in our realm of influence, those assigned to us by our generational curses, our own sin, and by God as intercessor for others. As we face them with the Word of God and the character of God, our vocation as overcomers will bring God's Kingdom to earth.

At the end of the story I see a few things that caused Job to overcome.
1. Job's education and acknowledgement of who God was.
2. His own repentance for his own self-sufficiency and underestimating who God was.
3. His worship and declaration of who God was in the face of evil.
4. His personal encounter with God; seeing God face to face.

Job 2:8-10 says,

8 And he took for himself a potsherd with which to scrape himself while he sat in the midst of the ashes.

9 Then his wife said to him, "Do you still hold fast to your integrity? Curse God and die!"

10 But he said to her, "You speak as one of the foolish women speaks. Shall we indeed accept good from God, and shall we not accept adversity?" In all this Job did not sin with his lips.

Job's wife had given up, but not Job.

Job continued to trust in God's character, at least to the extent that he knew God.

Job 2:11-13 says,

11 Now when Job's three friends heard of all this adversity that had come upon him, each one came from his own place--Eliphaz the Temanite, Bildad the Shuhite, and Zophar the Naamathite. For they had made an appointment together to come and mourn with him, and to comfort him.

12 And when they raised their eyes from afar, and did not recognize him, they lifted their voices and wept; and each one tore his robe and sprinkled dust on his head toward heaven.

13 So they sat down with him on the ground seven days and seven nights, and no one spoke a word to him, for they saw that his grief was very great."

Job's friends had come from far countries.

Job was famous internationally. Judging by the story, it seems that Job and his friends had adapted a sort of orthodoxy about their theology. Their faith, in who God was, had similar beliefs.

However, as we will see in later passages of Scripture, Job had to, in effect, say to them, "Look, I know what we thought we believed, but that stuff is not working now." They maintained that their orthodoxy was correct and that Job was wrong. They thought that the only reason Job was suffering was that he had hidden sin.

What they all found out later was, it was not hidden sin, it was their hidden sinful nature that God was trying to cleanse them from, and at the same time give Satan the black eye of vengeance!

Job 3:1-26 says,

> *1 After this Job opened his mouth and cursed the day of his birth.*
>
> *2 And Job spoke, and said:*
>
> *3 "May the day perish on which I was born, And the night in which it was said, 'A male child is conceived.'*
>
> *4 May that day be darkness; May God above not seek it, Nor the light shine upon it.*
>
> *5 May darkness and the shadow of death claim it; May a cloud settle on it; May the blackness of the day terrify it.*
>
> *6 As for that night, may darkness seize it; May it not rejoice among the days of the year, May it not come into the number of the months.*
>
> *7 Oh, may that night be barren! May no joyful shout come into it!*
>
> *8 May those curse it who curse the day, Those who are ready to arouse Leviathan.*

9 May the stars of its morning be dark; May it look for light, but have none, And not see the dawning of the day;

10 Because it did not shut up the doors of my mother's womb, Nor hide sorrow from my eyes.

11 "Why did I not die at birth? Why did I not perish when I came from the womb?

12 Why did the knees receive me? Or why the breasts, that I should nurse?

13 For now I would have lain still and been quiet, I would have been asleep; Then I would have been at rest

14 With kings and counselors of the earth, Who built ruins for themselves,

15 Or with princes who had gold, Who filled their houses with silver;

16 Or why was I not hidden like a stillborn child, Like infants who never saw light?

17 There the wicked cease from troubling, And there the weary are at rest.

18 There the prisoners rest together; They do not hear the voice of the oppressor.

19 The small and great are there, And the servant is free from his master.

20 "Why is light given to him who is in misery, And life to the bitter of soul,

21 Who long for death, but it does not come, And search for it more than hidden treasures;

22 Who rejoice exceedingly, And are glad when they can find the grave?

*23 Why is light given to a man whose way
is hidden, And whom God has hedged in?*

*24 For my sighing comes before I eat, And
my groanings pour out like water.*

*25 For the thing I greatly feared has come
upon me, And what I dreaded has happened
to me.*

*26 I am not at ease, nor am I quiet; I have
no rest, for trouble comes."*

**Here in Chapter 3, Job spills out his guts with the way he
really feels.**

In effect, he is charging God with some fault. Job regrets
that he was ever born. Some people say that this was wrong,
and is wrong today when we charge God with the way we
feel about things. However, I say, that to stuff and bury how
we really feel about God is to surely perish. If we feel and
think that God is being unjust, then we better get it out. I
believe that this was pleasing to God. In the end of the
Book, God said that He was pleased with what Job said, but
not with what his friends had said.

God is not pleased that we misjudge Him, but He is
pleased that we spill out our hearts before Him. When I do
that, I make sure that God understands and I understand, that
my "stuff" that is coming out is not a righteous judgment, but
sin. Then I can claim forgiveness and God's presence
results. I submit that to receive real revelation knowledge
from God, to hear Him speak personally to you, that you
must be totally gut level honest.

We need to be honest to hear from God.

Revelation knowledge comes from the resurrected Jesus,
through the Holy Spirit speaking, not contrary to, but
according to Scripture. He lets you know that He is tracking
with you and that He knows you. His rhema will nullify the

words of fear, condemnation and no hope in your life. However, we only reap what we sow; and in this case we must pour out our hearts to Jesus in order to experience His true companionship and presence.

Jesus told Peter about this as recorded in Matthew chapter 16:17. "Jesus answered and said to him, 'Blessed are you, Simon Bar-Jonah, for flesh and blood has not revealed this to you, but My Father who is in heaven.'"

The two disciples on the Road to Emmaus received revelation knowledge from the resurrected Christ. However, notice, that first Jesus had to extract from them their inner feelings, their unbelief. He asked them "What things." When He did that, He caused them to do like we all must do before receiving revelation knowledge, we must pour out our real feelings to the Lord, then He can work. They expressed their grief and disbelief. Jesus asked them in Luke 24:19 "What things (are you sad about)?" Jesus knew why they were sad, but He needed them to express their feelings.

After that, Jesus preached the Scriptures to them, showing them how He was offered as the Lamb of God for the blood covenant, and how He was now alive and speaking life to them.

Anonymous quote.

"Speak to Him, thou, for He hears, and Spirit with Spirit shall meet. Closer is He than breathing, and nearer than hands and feet." According to Tennyson's lines it is a very simple thing to find God. He is near at hand; speak to Him! Would that it were as easy as that. But for most of us the reality and nearness of God is a "discovery." An illustration of this "discovery" is found in the Book of Job. It is the cry of a baffled man

*who finds his inherited religion insufficient.
He cried, "O that I knew where I might find
Him."   Then follows the everlasting quest;
and the great "discovery"; "I have heard of
You by the hearing of the ear, But now my eye
sees You."*

*Oh, it is a monumental moment in any life
when the eyes of the spirit come open and
"hearsay" religions give place to the first
hand experience of the Presence.*

Job was really suffering.

We will look at his attitudes and his friend's discussions.
This ordeal was not just some "hangnail" or irritation in Job's
life, he was really suffering. He had lost all of his children to
an early death, all of his possessions, his entire ranch and all
of his animals were gone. Now Job was stricken with a
horrible sickness. He had boils from head to foot. He was in
constant pain with no relief.

"So I have been allotted months of futility, And
wearisome nights have been appointed to me. When I lie
down, I say, 'When shall I arise, And the night be ended?'
For I have had my fill of tossing till dawn. My flesh is caked
with worms and dust, My skin is cracked and breaks out
afresh. "My days are swifter than a weaver's shuttle, And are
spent without hope. Oh, remember that my life is a breath!
My eye will never again see good" (Job 7:3-7).

Tearing one's robe is the sign of a funeral. Job's friends came to a funeral.

"Now when Job's three friends heard of all this adversity that
had come upon him, each one came from his own place--
Eliphaz the Temanite, Bildad the Shuhite, and Zophar the
Naamathite. For they had made an appointment together to

come and mourn with him, and to comfort him. And when they raised their eyes from afar, and did not recognize him, they lifted their voices and wept; and each one tore his robe and sprinkled dust on his head toward heaven. So they sat down with him on the ground seven days and seven nights, and no one spoke a word to him, for they saw that his grief was very great" (Job 2:11-13).

For seven days they kept silent, then their theology kicked in.

What was their formula for suffering? You reap what you sow. Right? The righteous are always blessed. Right? Only the wicked suffer the curse, they thought. Therefore Job, you must be in some secret sin. God is punishing you they inferred. You must be some sort of a hypocrite Job.

Job looks through their talk and thinks, "Look, I don't understand this, but I trust God and I am not in some hidden sin." The three friends were being religious in their advice. Job had once been like this, but now he is not. God does not want us hooked into religious habits, He wants us hooked into real time face-to-face contact with Him!

Job was saying, "Our religion was wrong." It is not working as we thought.

Bildad always appealed to tradition. Zophar was shouting a call to repent. Job was saying, "My creed is gone. I need to know who God is!"

Doubt is not unbelief. It is faith growing up. Doubt becomes faith. But you have to take what you believe and apply it and allow it to be proven.

These friends were about to reap what they had sown, judgment.

They were sowing judgment without knowledge upon Job. When we do that, it is dangerous. Life and humans are too complicated for us to make judgments. The New Testament is clear, not to judge lest we be judged. Our job is to exhort, to encourage, and let the Holy Spirit do the convicting. Certainly God makes exceptions, but you better be very sure that God is speaking to you before you rebuke another.

Fear surely is an invitation to the enemy.
"For my sighing comes before I eat, And my groanings pour out like water. For the thing I greatly feared has come upon me, And what I dreaded has happened to me. I am not at ease, nor am I quiet; I have no rest, for trouble comes" (Job 3:24-26). However I have seen people make this verse the very doctrine of *why* Job suffered. If he just had more faith they argue, then Job would have stayed blessed. Wrong! Job was a man who God had on the path of knowing Him personally. Job was not there yet. He did not yet know about perfect love, which does cast away fear. While it is true that we need to fight fear like fire with God's perfect love, Job's fear was not the true bottom line of the story.

Job pursued his harsh talk.
"He tears me in His wrath, and hates me; He gnashes at me with His teeth; My adversary sharpens His gaze on me" (Job 16:9). "My spirit is broken, My days are extinguished, The grave is ready for me" (Job 17:1). In many of Job's outcries there resounds the voice of accusation that God is responsible for his suffering, and at the same time he declares his trust in God.

"Oh, that I might have my request, That God would grant me the thing that I long for! That it would please God to crush me, That He would loose His hand and cut me off!" (Job 6:8,9).

"I loathe my life; I would not live forever. Let me alone, For my days are but a breath" (Job 7:16).

"Have I sinned? What have I done to You, O watcher of men? Why have You set me as Your target, So that I am a burden to myself? Why then do You not pardon my transgression, And take away my iniquity? For now I will lie down in the dust, And You will seek me diligently, But I will no longer be" (Job 7:20,21).

"If I called and He answered me, I would not believe that He was listening to my voice. For He crushes me with a tempest, And multiplies my wounds without cause" (Job 9:16,17).

"I am blameless, yet I do not know myself; I despise my life. It is all one thing; Therefore I say, 'He destroys the blameless and the wicked'" (Job 9:21,22).

"For He is not a man, as I am, That I may answer Him, And that we should go to court together. Nor is there any mediator between us, Who may lay his hand on us both" (Job 9:32,33).

Feelings are real, and God only deals with real people.

However, we should not be governed by our feelings, and at the same time we should not be ashamed of them before God. That was the Puritan's problem. They adapted the pagan stoic principle of being unmoved by life. Many cultures are like Puritans. They feel that their strength is in the controlling of their emotions.

As I mentioned earlier, God needs our honest confession. "If we confess our sins, He is faithful and just to forgive us our sins and to cleanse us from all unrighteousness" (1 John 1:9). Stuffing our real feelings does not give God the license to work in our lives. Truth is always the delivering factor. Ugly truth is difficult to express, especially to God, but if you feel it you better give it to Him.

His friends warned him not to talk to God in that manner.
"How long will you speak these things, And the words of your mouth be like a strong wind?" (Job 8:2).

"If you were pure and upright, Surely now He would awake for you, And prosper your rightful dwelling place" (Job 8:6).

However God was pleased. "And so it was, after the LORD had spoken these words to Job, that the LORD said to Eliphaz the Temanite, 'My wrath is aroused against you and your two friends, for you have not spoken of Me what is right, as My servant Job has'" (Job 42:7).

David followed this principle with God and it paid off.
Just read the Psalms and you will find why David had a heart after God. He was real with God. When we sow our truth, we will reap God's truth. When we are real with God He will become real to us. That is our greatest need as it was Job's. I believe there is great value in reading five Psalms every day. In them God will link David's emotions with ours and we can experience being real and being healed.

Job's self-righteousness. Look at what he said.
"Yield now, let there be no injustice! Yes, concede, my righteousness still stands!" (Job 6:29).

"My righteousness I hold fast, and will not let it go; My heart shall not reproach *me* as long as I live" (Job 27:6).

"I put on righteousness, and it clothed me; My justice was like a robe and a turban" (Job 29 14).

"So these three men ceased answering Job, because he was righteous in his own eyes" (Job 32 1).

"Moreover Elihu answered and said: 'Do you think this is right? Do you say, 'My righteousness is more than God's'?'" (Job 35:1,2).

Later, Job found out the real righteousness.

Job 36:3 we will fetch my knowledge from afar; I will ascribe righteousness to my Maker.

Job obtained a vision of the Cross.

"Then He is gracious to him, and says, 'Deliver him from going down to the Pit; I have found a ransom'; His flesh shall be young like a child's, He shall return to the days of his youth. He shall pray to God, and He will delight in him, He shall see His face with joy, For He restores to man His righteousness" (Job 33:24-26).

Job answers his friends.

"But you forgers of lies, You are all worthless physicians. Oh, that you would be silent, And it would be your wisdom!" (Job 13:4,5).

"Your platitudes are proverbs of ashes, Your defenses are defenses of clay" (Job 13:12).

Amazingly, Job continued with a real trusting sort of faith for and in God, especially considering how little he knew about Him and especially since he had not really "met" Him.

"Though He slay me, yet will I trust Him. Even so, I will defend my own ways before Him" (Job 13 15).

Rebellion says, "God you are not doing a good job. I would do it different." But Job does not say that. He in effect says, "I don't like this, You are being bad to me, but in the end I trust You." Job has no evidence that God is with him, only that God is against him. "Though He slay me, yet will I trust Him. Even so, I will defend my own ways before Him" (Job 13:15).

God was luring Satan into a battlefield of defeat and Job into a realm of blessing beyond his imagination.

After Job had become real with God, after he realized that his righteousness was as filthy rags, after Job realized his religious beliefs about God were flawed, after God gave him a glimpse of who He, God, was, Job's heart was open to really see God face to face. God spoke to Job in a way that Job had never experienced before. God revealed Himself to Job. Job then saw himself in a different light; he no longer had any self-righteousness.

The day of seeing God finally came!
Job's greatest blessing was in seeing God face to face. God made Himself spiritually visible to Job.
"Then Job answered the LORD and said: 'I know that You can do everything, And that no purpose of Yours can be withheld from You. You asked, 'Who is this who hides counsel without knowledge?' Therefore I have uttered what I did not understand, Things too wonderful for me, which I did not know. Listen, please, and let me speak; You said, 'I will question you, and you shall answer Me.' "I have heard of You by the hearing of the ear, But now my eye sees You. Therefore I abhor myself, And repent in dust and ashes'" (Job 42:1-6).

Satan no longer had any weapons left.
Job had hung on to God. Job had allowed God to have His way in his life. Job was an overcomer. Job repented. Job humbled himself. Job in effect, took up his cross. Job had become a warrior for God, putting Satan where he belongs.
"... for God resists the proud, But gives grace to the humble. Therefore humble yourselves under the mighty hand of God, that He may exalt you in due time" (1 Peter 5:5b-6).

The Lord "turned the captivity" of Job.

"And the LORD turned the captivity of Job, when he prayed for his friends: also the LORD gave Job twice as much as he had before" (Job 42:10, KJV).

To "turn" the captivity means that the Lord recompensed Satan for what Satan had done to Job. It was turned, and Job received twice as much as he had before. But the biggest thing was now he had seen God face to face, and had an authentic relationship with Him. He did not have to trust in a doctrine like he had been doing with his friends.

God caused Job's friends to come to Job with a very formal burnt offering so that His wrath against them would be satisfied. They had to come to Job so that Job could pray for them and bring them into a right relationship with God.

Job ended up with double the livestock and other "stuff" that he had lost. He gained seven more children, which was the only loss that had not doubled. Why? Because his first set of children were in Heaven, so in effect, he *had* double.

Now that Job had been through "death and resurrection," Satan no longer had dominion over his life, his children and his "stuff." He was enjoying resurrection life.

Are you afflicted?

Get on God's path to knowing Him better and He will "turn" your captivity into real purpose in life. Best of all, get ready to "see Him" face-to-face!

Afflictions are a secret weapon.

"I now rejoice in my sufferings for you, and fill up in my flesh what is lacking in the afflictions of Christ, for the sake of His body, which is the church" (Colossians 1:24.)

Throughout the Bible, and especially in the Book of Revelation, we see that overcoming afflictions accomplish these major things.

1. Overcoming brings you closer to God. Revelation 21:7.

2. Overcoming sends demons in your realm of influence to an early retirement. It defeats strongholds, generational curses and demonic rulers. Revelation 20:3.

3. Overcoming brings an anointing in your life that sets others free. Revelation 20:4, 22:2.

4. Overcoming puts Jewels into the foundation of God's Kingdom. Revelation 21.

5. Overcoming anoints you to minister to others. Revelation 22.

The omnipresence, the omniscience of God.
When Job beheld who God was, his questions were answered. All that nature is, like the stuff we are made of, things we can see, that is our nursery school.

He is the creator. He had no beginning. He existed forever.

We cannot grasp eternity but we can see creation. God is not only the maker, but also the upholder, as he showed Job.

The key word in this Book is "know." Job, do you know?

I can trust God for what I don't understand. How?

By our trials we are brought face to face with God, if we live like Job did. By that seeing, we worship. By that worship we are coming against evil, declaring who He is.

We are called to the vocation of being Overcomers. He (often) does not remove evil, but calls us to overcome it. His grace is sufficient.

Like Paul said: "Oh death, where is they sting?" 1 Corinthians 15:55

From <u>Reaching Toward the Heights</u> Richard Wurbrand Founder of The Voice of the Martyrs.[4]

There is an old Christian story, kept in secrecy for the elect only. They hear it from a man or from an angel only in moments of supreme suffering.

A believer had devoted his whole life to seeking revelation in nature, in the faces of men, and within his own heart. He sought the sense of the ineffable name Jehovah. Approaching old age, he was condemned for his faith and was to be devoured by a leopard.

While waiting in the arena of the circus, he observed through the iron bars the wild beast to which he had been assigned for food. He gazed at the spots of its skin, and behold, a wonder. The rhythm of their design and their pattern explained to him the sense of the name of God for which he had been seeking for decades. At once he understood why he had to be sentenced to this cruel death. It was because this was the only means to fulfill his great wish. God had granted him this meeting with the leopard being the secret.

The martyr knew then that such a death was no death.

We all will be swallowed up by death in some manner. The question is, "What have you been looking for in life?" If you have looked for the right thing, death will reveal to you the mystery, and it will be just a veil

---

[4] Wurmbrand, Richard, *Reaching Toward The Heights*, Living Sacrifice Books, Bartlesville, OK 1979.

through which you will enter into the presence of the Lord. This applies not only to death, but also to every great suffering. Seek in its forms the name of God.

You Are Everything. A song by Brian Doerksen
My soul is yeaning for Your living streams;
My heart is aching for You,
All that I long for is found in Your Heart,
You are everything I need.
You are the thirst, You are the streams,
You are the hunger living deep inside of me.
You are the food that satisfies,
You are the provisions for the journey of our lives.
You are everything - You are.

Other titles by Larry Chkoreff

Grow or Die
Free To Be You
Has Your King Died?
Junk to Jewels
Be Real With God
The Blood of The Everlasting Covenant
Living By Faith In A Broken World
Job's Journey
Thorns to Fruit

Who Is The Lamb?
Is There A New World Coming?
A Vision for Marriage
Hearing God's Voice
The Psalms One Business Owner
Speak The Word.
Power Team for Kids (download)
Leadership – The Secret

www.ingramcontent.com/pod-product-compliance
Lightning Source LLC
Chambersburg PA
CBHW060648030426
42337CB00018B/3505